SHARKS!

PHONICS

All About Sharks

Book 1: sh (Beginning blend)

By Quinlan B. Lee

Photo Credits: cover: Matt9122/Shutterstock; title page: Steven Benjamin/iStockphoto; pages 2-3: Matt9122/Shutterstock; pages 4-5: Brian J. Skerry/Getty Images; pages 6-7: Water Frame/Alamy; page 8: Norbert Probst/Corbis; pages10-11: Becca Saunders/Minden Pictures; pages12-13: Swimwitdafishes/Dreamstime.com; pages14-15: Mark Conlin/Alamy; page16: qldian/iStockphoto.

ISBN 978-0-545-74698-4

12 11 10 9 8 7 6 5 4 3 2 1   14 15 16 17 18/0

Printed in China   145

First Printing, September 2014

SCHOLASTIC INC.

Sharks live in every sea in the world.
Some **sharks** live near the **shore** where it is **shallow**.

Some **sharks** live where it is deep.

Sharks are all different sizes.
A whale **shark** is huge!
This **shows** how big
the whale **shark** is.

Look at the diver!

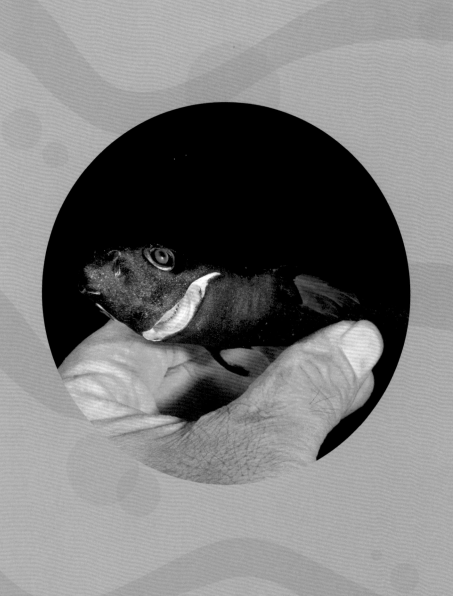

A pygmy **shark** is small!
It can be as small as a **shoe**.
This pygmy **shark** can also
shine in the dark.

Sharks are all
different **shapes**.
This is a hammerhead **shark**.
Its nose is **shaped** like
a **shovel**.

This is a longnose saw **shark**.
It is a **short shark** with a
long nose.
It has lots of **sharp** teeth in
a row like a saw.

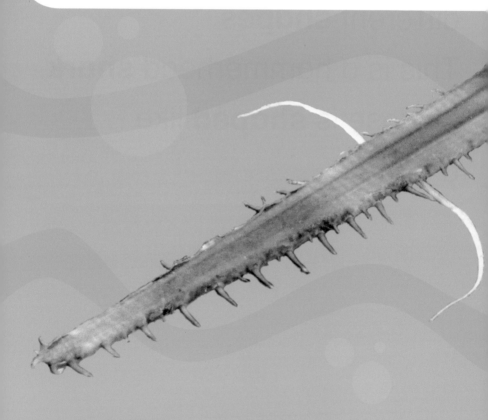

All **sharks** have lots of **sharp** teeth.
Some **sharks** have big **sharp** teeth.

Some **sharks** have small teeth that cut like saws.

Sharks can hurt people.
But people can also hurt
sharks!
Some **sharks** die in fish nets.
Some **sharks** are
shot for food.

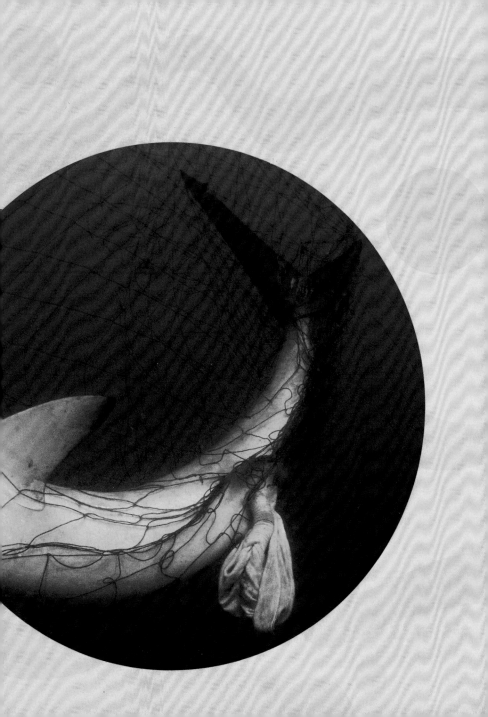

We must learn to **share** the seas with **sharks**.